Wordart 15-32

Eddie Brett.

COCKNEY
PIRATE
STUDIOS

Copyright © 2024 Eddie Brett
Cockney Pirate Studios
All rights reserved.
ISBN: 9798880280940
Imprint: Independently published

DEDICATION

My parents, TDUK, family and friends.

Ed Drewett and Olly Murs thanks for continuing to inspire me within your sphere of creativity and encouraging conversations.

Vincent, forever with me in spirit through this journey of life.

"To be a well-favoured man is the gift of fortune, but to write or read comes by nature."

William Shakespeare
Much ado about nothing- act 3 scene 3

This quote upon me did strike a chord. My grandad Fred was born in Elephant and castle, which is located on the south side of the river Thames in London. His parents were salt of the earth folk, Great grandad a slate roofer and my great grandmother a cleaner for theatres in the Westend. Busy earning a crust to keep the family unit fed, it would seem education and stimulation wasn't necessarily on the top of the agenda and so grandads' prospects weren't gifted to him; leaving school with poor writing skills and unable to read, he'd also picked up a criminal record to boot for stealing tools from someone's shed.

He met my grandma during an adolescent foray to Pontins in Weymouth. Upon their return he'd write to her (writing letters was a thing back in the day before text messaging). She recalls them needing much decryption to be remotely understandable but I've no doubt they were the affectionate doting words of Chaucer. Her dad, my great grandad was also born in Elephant and Castle and worked his way to becoming a respected detective in the Metropolitan Police Service working on many cases including the gang violence of The Krays. An interesting point to note is that historically, young families of police officers had the opportunity to live in service accommodation above police stations and other public buildings and so my grandma was born and lived for a time in Pentonville Prison, Kings Cross, London.

My Grandma, nervous upon presenting her new boyfriend due to his familiarities with the alternate side of the law eventually fessed up to her father – who being born from the same cloth was sympathetic – exclaiming to a relieved daughter 'most boys in that area are on probation for something.' And went on to fess up himself that he already knew because he'd conducted a background check upon first hearing about him. When my great grandad George found out that he struggled with literacy, he paid for him to attend evening school and in short taught him how to read. In my lifetime I never knew my Grandad without a book on the go, and when I say books, I mean huge meaty novels. A man of few possessions he owned a large bookshelf proudly displaying his conquests like personal trophies. He also had an appetite for fiction history and geography, and I've no doubt his copies of Michael Palin's travel memoirs had a huge influence on my brother Travel Dave UK who, as I write this, resides on a boat heading to Antarctica.

Words, when writing offer a freedom of expression and when reading allow us to escape, learn and connect. Words allow us to travel whilst being still. Words give ideas life beyond the tongue. They can be chiselled and refined like sculpting. Toyed with. They exist. Born from the mind and given to the world. There is a human craving and insatiable desire to both tell and hear stories.

'I love answering questions because If I don't tell you, all that I know goes with me.' Grandma Sue

Wordart 15-32

CONTENTS

	origin	I
1	Crying in my sleep	Pg 21
2	Dream	Pg 22
3	A love poems poem	Pg 24
4	Bus m8	Pg 26
5	Figure of 8	Pg 28
6	Honest	Pg 36
7	Bellyful	Pg 40
8	Stars	Pg 41
9	Peace and love	Pg 42
10	Alcohol (Myself)	Pg 48
11	Fame	Pg 50
12	Hug	Pg 52
13	Be yourself	Pg 53
14	Big ideas start small	Pg 54
15	Time	Pg 55
16	Bread	Pg 56
17	Cooked Breakfast	Pg 57
18	Wank	Pg 59
19	After Wank	Pg 62
20	Vinyl flooring	Pg 63
21	Reflection	Pg 64

22	I can't get no sleep	Pg 65
23	Snore	Pg 66
24	Create new password	Pg 68
25	Internet mark ii	Pg 70
26	E.T. put phone away	Pg 72
27	Moaning	Pg 73
28	I don't care but I do	Pg 74
29	Understand parents, understand theirs	Pg 75
30	Yonder	Pg 76
31	Dear Dad	Pg 77
32	Harry Kane	Pg 78
33	Loneliness	Pg 80
34	Mountains and Sea	Pg 82
35	Onlyplans Mars	Pg 84
36	Sinking	Pg 87
37	War	Pg 88
38	Have a drink	Pg 90
39	Waltham Forest	Pg 92
40	Seed	Pg 95
41	Baldy	Pg 97
42	Lists	Pg 99
43	Love	Pg 101

ORIGIN

Wordart. The first dip into graphic design for any budding creative wanting to express themselves beyond black and white Times New Roman was using wordart. An important decision made either at the beginning or end of every word-processed document. Choosing from a list of pre-programmed fonts, and deciding how to make the title pop.

  In the 2000s I can't begin telling you just how exciting this was, each one said a little something about the person using it and we all had our go to selections... Subconsciously piecing together our personal brand identities in an IT classroom. They say that human beings change their personalities every 7 years; well, this used to be my choice:

Wordart 15-32

And I think this is what I would choose now:

Wordart 15-32

I'm sure a psychiatrist could tell you a lot of interesting stuff about what the change in font says about me and how my personality has evolved over the years. However, I have never visited a psychiatrist. I've thought about it and I've been told to many times, sometimes sympathetically and sometimes in rage from the spout of angry people or parents but in all honesty I've never felt the need because fortunately when I need understanding or explanation, exploration or a decluttering of thought – that is when I head to pen and paper (or laptop keyboard) There's a symbiotic relationship between my mind, emotions and words. I find great joy from creating something that otherwise would never of existed. Writing is my gateway to understanding things and myself.

There are no rules with words. Good is good. Understanding is the only true requirement if you are wanting to tie notice to a recipient. Understanding feeds from delivery and explanation. Education and academics try to govern retrospective patterns and best practices, but this is only ever a highway to comprise uniformity and easy understanding for mass consumption. It's non enforceable. A word's relevance derives from use, not architecture. Words will change and adapt, meaning will evolve and adopt additional purpose. The history of the land and its culture entwined within the language of the day. Accent, tone, and slang boast data beyond just understanding and push the pallet of language towards a symphony of identity. Words and language are choices. We carve out who we are and who we want to be with words. There are no rules but there are customs.

Songs are loud poems. Melody plonked above rhythmic timing. Timing is something that I had to work on in the early stages of my life with help from bandmates and producers because everything I was presenting was extremely wordy and so sometimes an element of shaping was needed to fit certain ideas into pleasing melodic phrases. Love Sick Mark 1 was a scatter gun of verse lyrics and because each line was performed to a single strummed chord it was pretty wild and in some respects that was its own vibe… That's the beauty of art, there are no right answers, just decisions to make. I know the first producers we worked with (Red Triangle) loved that it was so free because they'd never heard anything like it. A song that every time performed was slightly different. A monologue of words in the verse and then bam! Snapped into a rigid fast paced unified chorus. It was only when we went on the telly that we had to amend it to fit specific timing for a backing track. I liked the changes, it gave it a nice flow, it wasn't a raw artistic decision previously, it was a lack of knowledge and skill lol. But as I said, sometimes that sense of creative necessity offers a raw authenticity that cannot be replicated, and it is that that doth be the spice.

When someone shares that something you've written has had a profound impact on them and their life… Honestly, it's the greatest gift of all. I wonder if Paul McCartney still gets a buzz from this or whether it just blends in to the normality of the day. It doesn't happen with everything but when you know, you know. There's a poem called Dream and a song called Honest which spring to mind. My work is yet to receive the reach that I feel destined, however my experiences thus far offer an optimism and sense of mission. Writing has given me a sense of purpose.

My fascination for story-telling sizzled around the campfire. I was fully involved with the Scouts growing up; Beavers, Cubs, Scouts, Explorer Scouts… I lived a double life in my teens because it was so uncool at school to knowingly be in the Scouts. Dare I self-declare I was quite a popular lad? I was funny, and funny universally transcends social groups. I had to keep my Scouting life a secret because kids are cruel, it's 'eat or be eaten'. Any sliver of knowledge that sets you outside of the norm could be used as a rod to pierce through your back. The 'cool kids' will never understand the 'nerds' and the 'nerds' would never entertain the company of the 'cool kids' but gratefully, varied interests have afforded me the ability to surf between social groups. Too unstable to find grounding, too ambitious to keep still.

My immediate family separated in my teens, and we all formed new lives in different directions and so I feel both attached and detached from an orthodox family unit in equal measures. I was fortunate growing up that other households took me under their wing as and when I needed to feel some convention. At heart I feel like a stray dog and thereby lies my inability to commit to jobs, relationships, locations, and gym memberships. Having said all this life and my immediate family set up has never felt calmer and more together than it does at this moment in time and so maybe now, hopefully I might find some chill. Although I fear Pandora's box of emotional puzzle pieces has been tipped out too belligerent and sparsely to truly connect a lasting portrait of unity. But amidst my education in acting and theatre we can at least yield the tools to pretend.

    Maybe the unwavering relationship I have with following my gut is a good thing? It doesn't always feel that way, but I don't think society could ever be seen to fully support the unusual as mass organisation relies on predictability. The world however does need weirdos and misfits to mix the day up and offer perspective. Inspire the lost, and reassure the comforted. I'm pretty invested in all this writing and performance lark by this point and so I guess I'll just keep smiling and trucking on. The gift of the rambling man is the fresh wind that flows past as he walks.

    Anyway, back to campfires…. Stories connect. Whether round a campfire, listening to songs, watching films, POEMS, plays, or fables steeped in loose truths told down the pub. A compelling storyteller can be intoxicating and demand ears. The fear of missing out exists amongst whispers… Shh! When I was a kid, we used to go to a campsite called Gilwell Park which is the Wembley Stadium of Scouting and it just so happened to be located in the town in which I grew up. Meaning, I could frequently frequent. The campfires were magical! Large, tall, roaring beasts swallowing timber pallets. SeaWorld throw fish down the gullets of dolphins – well at Gilwell, logs get safely risk accessed and placed in the belly of the flame. Sending a warm orb around those present. A sloped venue with wooden benches cascading surrounded the fire pit. In your head picture the coliseum in Rome shrunk and built from left over materials found in your Grandads' tool shed, very Robin Hood tree house vibes… cosy, damp, submerged, intimate, placed within the encompass of trees. The sort of place goblins and fairies would happily call home and the perfect place to tell stories and sing songs. The energy was always jubilant and optimistic, regardless of the weather. People from around the world, of all ages united to share a unique Gilwell campfire experience. I would observe the performances and song choices like a critic, trying to dissect understanding amongst what captivated and what lost momentum.

I present 'Edo's 2024 top tips for performing campfire songs':
- Unique, individual flair/style- charisma
- Confidence
- Knowing the lines fluently
- Participation with audience
- Volume and vocal clarity
- Costume/ look/ fashion.
- A story that reveals a surprise

Whether an overweight Viking from Finland or a mousey introverted computer geek from California, this circle welcomed the endearingly interesting. People came to have fun, they wanted to have fun and they wanted each daring candidate to succeed and deliver to the occasion.

It's never not scary performing, no matter how often you do it, whether it's karaoke or the o2 arena… the nerves will kick in and we must overcome them. Breathing, remembering to enjoy it (even if you lie to yourself), practicing (well beforehand!) and then just constantly flexing that muscle… The only time I didn't feel anything before going on a stage was when I stopped caring, I was drained, I was over the whole experience and that's when I knew it was time for a break.

Eventually I was ready to step up to the campfire stage. I must have been about 12, I decided to go with: baby shark do do do do do (20 years before it blew up on tiktok lol)... It was melodic, easy, silly, and fun and I'd think of new types of sharks and actions to include to give it its own spin to any other version. I'd look around at people giggling and singing, moving, dancing, smiling, being together, being in the moment. That is the feeling I've been chasing ever since.

There is the performer and there are the words... Two individual things. I don't subscribe to the snobbery around needing to do both... great is great. We should lean in wherever our skills lie and heed collaboration whenever we need support... Although I guess my style is that of a folk pen-to-tongue kinda journeyman, nothing about me is supposed to show or be the face of perfection, I'm supposed to show scars behind a smile, that is my story, I am not glitz and glam. There's an honesty to my approach and I'd do well to remind myself of that sometimes.

I'd been really into music for some time, really into it, it was proactive not passive, I heard heavy metal and loud guitars and that was it! I'd record all the music videos from KerrangTV or MTV2 to VHS (a physical tape we used to stream stuff from), draw the artwork of albums, write out lyrics to songs. I fully wanted to be a rockstar, but I couldn't play guitar and so was left feeling frustrated and helpless looking at my Christmas present knowing I couldn't learn any songs. The blunt reality was that the lack of knowledge paired with my desperate hunger forced me to write my own songs... My mum's friend Peter gave me a guitar chord book which told you where to put your fingers and so I started to teach myself a few chords... I was armed with 4 chords, 'that sounds nice' I thought. I now know that I was playing a 'major chord progression in the key of C' but at the time I just navigated that those finger shapes in that sequence sounded cool. What now?? How do people write? What do they write about? How do they approach it? I'm sure there are lots of books explaining some instructions and my dad would share some with me but honestly it winds me up. If you read a book about how to write you are learning to write like that person and not yourself... There's enough good stuff out there to never need anything new and so we must add to the pot, we owe it to the pot to be individual and so allow instinct to guide you. With that said, each to their own, if a book works for you read the book... I know Mike Skinner wrote his albums utilising a book he'd read about song writing.

    My Grandad Fred passed away. I was shopping for a suit for his funeral in Marks and Spencer's when my mum received a phone call. It's the maddest thing because I knew what she was going to tell me before she even opened her mouth. I'd picked it up from her tone of voice, her eyes, the way she was looking at me, the change from the excitement of hearing from someone to a complete collapse of pain and guilt. That is when I found out my best friend from primary school, Vincent, had also died.
    We were 15. His mum asked me to tell everyone at school and so I did, and I felt like an evil wizard with the ability to make people cry instantly... I'd open my mouth and wham, hugs, and tears straight away... I found the reactions surprising at first as I hadn't been crying, I wasn't prepared for that, but it made sense, I was confused, why I wasn't crying? I was still in shock, we don't always process things straight away, it was such a large thing to wrap my head round that my mind was saying we'll deal with that later. The day after my Grandad's funeral my mum, like an absolute champion, drove me to Scotland. Our destination a remote island called Uist. Getting there involved travelling over land and sea via plane, car, boat, and foot. It was the first time I'd been to Scotland, and my eyes gazed out the rental car window as we passed the beauty of green Corbett hills, grey Munros, blue lakes and ferocious dark seas. A world away from the suburban town we grew up in. Each boat we took got smaller as did the population of the destination. We knew we were near when people knew

the purpose of our visit. By the time we'd arrived the funeral had taken place, we'd spent a day travelling from one end of Britain to the other and his mum honestly couldn't quite believe we'd even made it at all, I think back to all the little random check points on our journey, pre Google Maps and I can't quite believe it either. Thanks Mum.

    We walked to the church yard; a fresh imprint of grass visible. His mum and my mum left so I could be by myself. I'd not seen a grave with someone's name on it who I knew. A bizarre first. It finally felt real, and the tears came. A begrudging acceptance that life doesn't always follow an age bound pattern. We'd grown up as little beings together, yet to fully blossom. Laughed, loved Arsenal, Iron Maiden, South Park, going to the park, more laughing, being silly, dressing my dog up in human clothes, the excitement of going to his house or having a friend at mine, we weren't old enough to be complicated yet and so all my memories with him were that of happiness… We are taught about how babies grow, then we learn, then we procreate, then they grow, then we get old and eventually die… The concept of life seems unfair even whilst following its conventional protocol so please, someone, explain this?! This isn't the way things go. And so, everything I'd learnt about life had to be relearnt.

    After primary school, we both went to different secondary schools and then Vincent moved to Scotland, he wrote down his address and phone number. Vince as he was now called by his Scottish friends, of which I couldn't resent because I'd swapped from Edward to Eddie called me up, I put the phone down at first because I thought it was a prank call. I didn't know anyone with a Scottish accent. He called again, and I listened a little longer eventually realising who it was. We laughed about his new accent, and I could hear his friends in the back laughing at mine. I think he wanted me to validate a story about something. Maybe about a boy called Harry cutting off a girl's ponytail when he was first given a pair of scissors in class, or Jack telling a teacher to F'off and running to hide in the boys toilets. That sort of thing maybe and so it was only a fleeting call and that was the last time I spoke to him...

When I came back from his funeral I went to my bedroom, and was confronted by his phone number and address written on a piece of paper on my computer table... And I just felt this compulsion to write. Without fear or over thinking I just wrote. That was my first experience of this, and honestly it wasn't me. I was there sure... but only as a vessel, the point between the wherever and the paper. I've felt like that about a lot of my words when they come together, a feeling that I'm just channelling something. I've thought this in silence for years and then as I've got older becoming curious about spirituality and religion, it begins to lend potential explanation. Even if it's all entirely bollox the idea of a spiritual companion is a lot more comforting than nothingness.

Songs are loud poems. I had the chords, I had the words and my first song was called 'Crying In My Sleep'.

After secondary school I went to Harlow College to study drama, when my friend Amber was leaving to go to a special musical theatre college, I followed her, and it was this song that I sung at the audition. The teacher at this college taught Matt Willis from Busted (she is Miss McKenzie in the song 'that's what I go to school for') 'Crying In My Sleep' enabled her to see a little bit of him in a little bit of me, enough to get me in to the college with a part scholarship. I remember mid audition the College secretary laughing at the 'Post-it note' lyric, I hadn't intended it to be funny so it caught me by surprise, but after I laughed thinking that she must spend so much time writing on Post-It notes to hear it used in a song made her feel seen. Funnily enough, I performed this song to Matt Willis and the rest of the college in my first year, when he came to visit, I think back now, and it must have been such an awkward thing to sit through for him lol! A depressing song nervously played on a novicely strummed guitar. Shelly cried though so maybe it packed a punch. Matt gave me his email address and said to email if I had any questions. That felt cool. Progress was being made towards becoming a rockstar.

Time for some poems

Crying In My Sleep

this is probably the most depressing thing that i ever say
i don't know why i find it drawing
it's a nightmare that is wrapped in mourning
i walked past the other day
by the graveside where your flowers lay
i keep an image in my mind
block out the bad, remember good times

not a day goes by when i don't think you
a feeling kept inside and i don't know what to do
shut it out and pretend it's not there?
but a life not knowing you i just couldn't bare

still have your details on a post-it note
at the time i didn't know what to write
but i should have wrote
it wasn't dislike it wasn't through spite
it was just my busy distant teenage mind
and my biggest regret still to date is;
even if i had the words, it would be too late
but i know you're listening way up high
and you've read every sentence that i've put by

still hear you crying in my sleep
still hear you whisper when i weep
still see your face in my dreams
you are the centre of my memories

Wordart 15-32

Dream

i'm having a midlife crisis at the tender age of just 18
and i had to ask myself 'what is my dream?'

and 'what is a dream?'

is it something to have and not to achieve?
just like a faith is to not know and to just believe
oh, why my creative mind can't be satisfied
with an nvq in building
and then an apprenticeship?
tis an honourable trade with respectable pay
and it's what most of my friends did
but i want more than this town
the glitz and the glam
and am trying to carve a career from a dream
but where can i get an a-level in chance?
a diploma in what if?
and a b-tec based on a whim?
if i don't see it through
then i'll never quite know
and it's this thought that right now makes my life so hard
will i work to great success?
i thrive to be the best!
and i can't accept that i wouldn't survive

this isn't a hobby
it's more than a past time
it frustrates me when people say it looks fun

calm down mate
you're forgetting why you do it...
if i make it look easy it's a job well done

so, i'll pull up my striped socks
belt out the top notes
and make my idols proud
touch wood if it doesn't work out
i'll just get a 9-5
and blend straight in with the crowd.

A Love Poems Poem

i wish my words were listened to with a rhythm
and a beat
and that i could discard televisions
out the windows of hotel retreats
i wish i could use my lyrics to travel and see the world
but instead, i'm stuck to this 2d page
and in the library i'm held

i get picked on for not being tough
like the thriller novels slash books
but i don't think it's fair to be compared to literature
based upon villains and crooks
i get on well with my science fiction pals
although i feel as if they befriend me
to get with the princesses in the fairy tales
i wish men would stop using me
for i do not want to be placed upon paper for eternity
my real passion being music
and to become a rock star my destiny.
portraying real emotion on stage my identity.

i could sell out wembley as well as borders
and get illegal downloads as well as pre-orders
but as it stands,
i have no hands, and this causes great torment
as i lack the ability to play an instrument
oh, if only i was in with the music magazines
but they're all cool and trendy
filed in the underground cabinet scenes

constantly gloating about how they are fluently educated
in lennon and mccartney
they have no idea that the beatles and love poems
are like family
but i am getting bitter and dusty
and can not be bothered to pull out my pages and disagree
so, i guess i'll quit chasing the dream and save my dignity

maybe a dream is something to have and not to achieve?
and this is something that a book cannot teach
but a love poem can try...

so maybe my fate remains here
between shakespeare and wilde
kept warm and dry
serving a duty to bring love and emotion
out of the receiving name
forever bearing only a vision
of the love poem
on the hard rock wall of fame.

Bus M8

on the bus home in a state of coma
again! that stale, sweaty aroma.
is there a rule:
'at least one person on public transport has to smell of piss'?
because this is a stereotype that i am willing to dismiss
z
    z
        z

i doze off to stunt the smell and i dream of being in a taxi
i don't have to change seats
and there's no one sitting next to me
no stops or old women moaning
no whining accents of girlfriends and boyfriends phoning
i would say that i don't have to listen to other people's
annoying chat chit
but. we all know that comes with a cabbie's banter, whit.
and that no journey is complete
without being updated on the latest:

- football
- fights
- tit

now as we glide through political topic to topic
and just previous of his chronologic opinion on pornography
he decides that this fare
with the client
would be a suitable time for him to dictate his autobiography.
i don't care if he didn't get on with school
and i don't care if once under his back seats he once found a
gram of cocaine, a mobile phone and a stanley knife
and i don't care if his fiancé ran away to australia with his
brother the day before she become his wife

it's not that i'm miserable nor a heartless soul
it's just i've been working hard all day
and my mind has taken its toll!
he waffles on about how he is grateful for his brother stopping
him marrying that troll
joining a family where he would loose his working class
heritage and become a toff
unaware in the back despite my best efforts
... i nod off...
z
    z
        z

and i dream about the cow jumping over the moon
and the spoon being whisked away by the fork
and i dream that just as i'd finished work
i'd decided to walk

Figure Of 8

mum can i stay in here please?
because i'm going to be born soon and to be honest,
i don't see the need
i've got warmth, shelter and this tube is a great feed...
you must admit it is a little bit selfish to assume
that i wanted to be a part of your creed
it's just i'm going to have to teach myself how to walk
and then as if it's not enough for me to be cute
you're gonna want me to talk
and then there's school and making new friends
i wont like the other kids but you'll make me pretend
because their parents are close with dad, and you mum!
and even though we have nothing in common
he's my new best chum
you see, he's in to garden bugs and worms
but they are disgusting and make my stomach churn
no, i'm not wasting my time with that childish stuff
because i have a vision, yes specific plans
it was only the other day,
that i painted di vinci's mona lisa with my hands

and then i'll grow
and learning gets harder
and then i'll grow even more and...
other things get harder.
and these yucky creatures known as girls
begin to enter my butterfly world
everything's great and you think you're in love!
but she's having sex with your best mate!
yes! the one with the bugs!

but i have a vision. specific plans.
and i will not let a girl get in my way
for i am to express myself through art
oh shit, i think i'm gay
you're not disappointed just a little surprised
but grandma was shocked
and dad still hasn't replied

then off to uni. who needs a family's support?
oh why was i born?!? it's your fucking fault!!!
i scream through the door as i leave the house
in my pocket a gram of cocaine and £20
yes, i know it wrong
but i'm hooked, to that magic white powder
where were you mum when i needed a shoulder?
what good is a letter every now and then?
don't worry, there's plenty of shoulders listening
where you'd call a crack den
but like frank says: 'the powder leads to the needle'
and the needle leads to you lying on a hospital bed
with a failing heart
then you and dad arrive
and it's just like the start... you remember...
you, dad, the doctor and me all in the same place
i don't think this world was made for me
now that i've had a taste
i didn't even get a painting up in the tate
i can't continue with this. not in this state
but luckily in the womb it's not to late
so i move
and as you feel me kicking
i tie the cord around my neck
in a figure of 8

The Story Continues...

This is a poetry book and so I don't want to just fill it up with song lyrics as that would be lazy... However, the truth is I pride myself on my words, and lyrics are words, and so it feels appropriate to include a few hand-picked sections. If you boiled my being in a large cauldron and left it to reduce, I'd hope that the matter left in whatever gunky form would be humour and words.

So, let's talk Love Sick... Love Sick is without a doubt the song that changed everything for me... Crying In My Sleep was super important as it's the song that got me in to college. And then, once at college I was gigging and jumping on any opportunity that came my way, performing in shops or open mike nights, anywhere I could get in front of a microphone and hopefully an audience. However they don't always go hand in hand. A lot of times there's just you, a mic, and an empty room but it is what it is... I had a handful of songs, enough for a short set and as previously stated I could never really do covers justice, so I was only really interested in writing my own songs. Whilst doing a gig in a clothes shop, I got super frustrated that everyone was just walking past me shopping and not paying attention to what I was saying. I mean the cheek of people to go clothes shopping and shop! But it made me wonder how to remove my cloak of invisibility. How do you grab people? How do comedians do it? They don't even play an instrument, yet everyone hangs on to every word and it's the words I care about... PUNCHLINES, comedians have stories that require you to listen throughout to understand the joke... This came naturally in my poems because I wanted the stories to go somewhere and have a pop, but I'd never considered introducing it to songs until Love Sick.

I was in the final of a competition called Jack Wills Unsigned, this was in 2010. I'd managed to get through to the final, however I felt like I'd only just scraped through the semi-final off the back of my personality winning the crowd over and not necessarily my music. Also, my mates were in the audience and being unfavourably loud compared to anyone else. Randomly, Bianca Gascoigne was also there… She was super nice to me and officially my first celebrity fan. I really wanted to win the competition as the judges were A&Rs from EMI (the record label that Iron Maiden was signed to) and when you don't know nothing about nothing as far as the music industry is concerned that seems to feel important. I wanted to write a new song, something fresh, so that if anyone from the previous show came to the final, they were presented with something new.

    I was at home, watching a documentary about Boy George and Culture Club. The relationship between George and the drummer, the love affair, the secrets and betrayal, the juxtaposition between life on the road compared to being back home amongst normality really hit me. The walls of reality blurred, the rules of work and friendship muddied and married with children thrown in just for shits and giggles… Alas, the creative juices started to flow, pen and paper grabbed, I used the same chords as Crying In My Sleep just strummed quicker… And then I decided to try and implement some moments of funny in case anyone dared not pay attention to me whilst I was performing…

> i was crumbled like apple pie
> when you left my flat only wearing a goodbye
> in your bag were my ralph lauren tops
> on your feet were my brand-new workout reeboks

Boom, opening lines that were fruity and playful. Surely, I'd have everyone's attention for the rest of the song now as they'd not want to miss any more giggle lyrics. I then went to college the next day and begged my friends Sonny and Te to sing it with me at the final of this competition. Explaining how I was up against a band, and I wanted the songs to feel more dynamic. They agreed quite willingly but said they didn't like the second verse, 'it was too dark, deep and unnecessarily depressing'. I've no idea what they were now despite remembering that feedback so vividly, but I came back the next day with new lyrics of which they approved, and we started to rehearse. Whilst bunking a jazz dance class we could hear the dreaded manic tapping of heeled shoes echoing through the corridor and this sound only ever belonged to one person. We stopped playing guitar and pretended to act nonchalant and purposeful although it was no use, Michelle Blair (our course director 'that's what I go to school for' Busted - Miss McKenzie) had already heard guitars and singing coming from studio 3 when there should definitely not have been any sound coming from studio 3. I can't remember the exact dialogue that followed but it was something along the lines of:

"What the f*#k are you doing in here and not Jazz! I don't care if it's not your thing, you show the teacher some f*#king respect and show up! This isn't your college; you don't get to just pick and choose what you do!! However, I did like what I heard so play it to me at the end of the day and if it's not amazing, you'll be in trouble'.

I know this sounds like something from a Roald Dahl book but it's legitimately what happened. I was nervous because technically speaking I wasn't even allowed to do gigs outside of the college nor auditions; reason being they wanted students completely focused on college stuff and extracurricular activities distract from that… However, Michelle allowed me to do gigs purely on the promise that it wouldn't interfere with my college work, and I remained punctual… And then here I was not only distracting myself from college work but two other students…

The method in Michelle's madness (which I only know now upon reflection), the reason we weren't expelled is that she was shaping the end of year show, a showcase for the third year students to get in front of agents and hopefully kickstart their careers. Now, big show moments involve scene and costume changes so you physically can't have back-to-back big moments with a full cast... and so filler moments; solos etc. get slotted in to allow everything to run effortlessly through. Variety is the spice of any good show, and a good show is the sum of the parts that make it up. Our moment of creative rebellion might have been of use to her. Later that day, Michelle heard Love Sick and thought it was brilliant and put it in the end of year show. The rest of the college were fuming because first years were lucky to even be in the show never mind having a feature especially when there were third year students that weren't even being graced with such a moment... but alas, that's showbiz baby, we were just relieved to not be told off for missing jazz...

We then headed to Jack Wills in Islington and won the 2010 JW unsigned competition; we didn't get a record deal from the EMI A&Rs, they really weren't bothered and gave us 'keep working hard' vibes although we did then get to play the 2010 JW Varsity Polo festival. After that we performed in the CPA college end of year show, Love Sick was clearly loved, and everyone kept asking us the same question 'What is the name of your band?!'... a conversation that had yet to take place but it was obvious that something was happening and so I popped the question. 'Fancy being in a band?' I remember Te needing some convincing but as I'm sure you may know he eventually agreed, and the Loveable Rogues were born.

The first song we wrote together as a band was 'Honest' – an absolute cracker. We wrote it with Rick and George from Red Triangle an amazing writing and production duo in Bournemouth. This was all pre BGT and a very exciting, wholesome time for us which I think is captured in the song. We did a lot of stuff with Red Triangle, and they've since gone on to do some amazing stuff with everyone from James Arthur to Green Day.

I love the title 'Honest'; I think it helped to establish the identity of what we were about. The song was written with our mums in mind to basically say 'chill, we've got this'. At that point we'd collectively decided to leave college in pursuit of the band and the dream despite us all pleading so hard to go to the college in the first place. I think they all thought we were mad, of which we definitely were, however sometimes life calls for those bold moments to stick a flag in the ground and say 'this is the direction, no turning back now!'

Honest

don't cry, try not to wait up for me tonight
i'm leaving for the future and it's bright
being swept off my feet like a drifting kite
and i'm regretting all the choices that i make
but i know that we can learn from our mistakes
with every single new step that we take

sit tight, i'm off around the world to do my thing
and every word you say, i'm listening
and when i wake up it'll just be me
don't cry, even when i'm distant, far away
and you're sitting, warm, by the fireplace
tears blur the embers, you'll see my face

i might repeat myself, am i a parrot?
you know how i feel and that's apparent
a final move to win or lose and i can't make you choose
it's up to you

and i told you my roots will keep me honest
i'll be a good boy, that i promise
if i said that i won't leave then i'll stay true
'cos i told you my roots will keep me honest
if there's a bus home, i'll be on it
when i told you i'm not leaving
you'll believe it when you see
i'm back for you

One of my favourite reviews/ comments I've ever read about myself said 'who rhymes "parrot" and "apparent"' lol!!! Brilliant.

> Don't cry, Even when I'm distant, far away
> And you're sitting, warm, by the fireplace
> Tears blur the embers, you'll see my face

This line sums up my memory of that song. We needed that final lyric, George and Te were in the studio working on the vocals, melody, and instrumentation. Me, Sonny, and Rick went for a walk hoping a change of scenery would spark something as we'd hit a wall. Rick's parents' house was gigantic, I remember us joking about it having two kitchens. We settled in their lounge and there was a beautiful rustic fireplace and I remember staring into it hoping to find answers. It reminded me of these blurry picture books my Grandad would collect inside newspapers, you stare at the random hazy patterns and eventually your eyes space out and it revealed an image that you can't see with the naked eye. With this, all these different connections snapped together in my mind and the lyrical puzzle was complete. I've always been good at certain stuff but never brilliant…lyrics however, they made me feel special… The look on Sonny and Rick's faces when I presented the line was like I'd just spunked out diamonds which was extremely gratifying and something I'd always get excited for, that smile of approval. I just remembered being stoked with the "tears blur the embers you'll see my face" it felt so visually satisfying.

The process of writing a song, the overall day and experience can have a huge impact sometimes on your relationship with it. That was a golden Loveable Rogues day. It had it all. Productive, fresh, belief, aspirational, it really felt like we were on to something. We were all so invested in its conception. A true team effort, ideas and opinions flowing from all and completely free of thinking about money or splits or what a label might say. We'd driven to Bournemouth, which was about 2 hours 20 minutes from Essex, wrote a banger, recorded it all and then drove back in the same day, and it's basically the same version you can listen to today. George burnt the track onto a CD and we listened to it on repeat on the way home in Sonny's Ford Fiesta which I must add was covered in the most outrageous boy racer orange stickers.

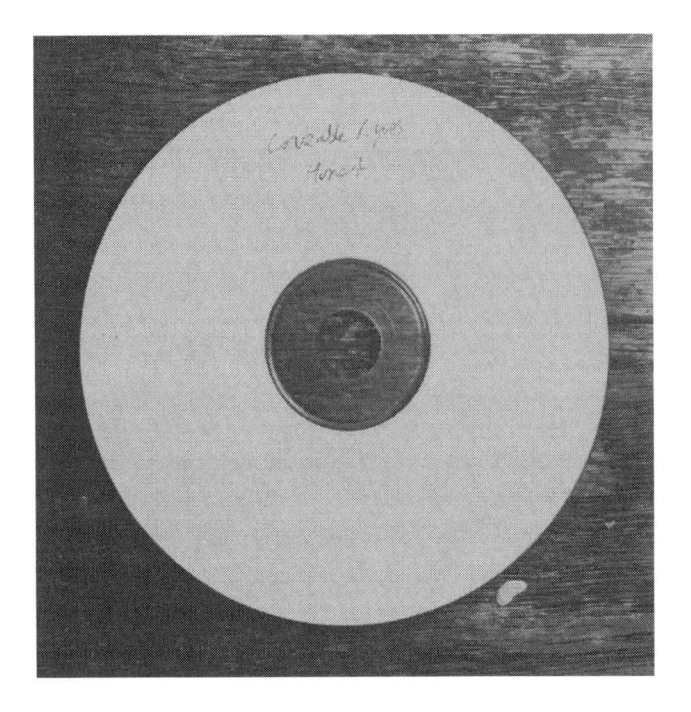

We did a cover of Bruno Mars' 'Lazy Song'. By this point life had all gone a bit crazy. I remembered a Bob Dylan interview I'd seen where he talks about how he sold his soul to the devil. I remember thinking, 'well if that's what it takes, I'd do that as well' Funny reflecting upon that now... Because words have power, actions have consequences... What's metaphoric, what's spiritual, what's sacred and what seeps into reality? I wrote a verse to spice up our cover as I guess that's what I used to do... Still reluctant to do covers I guess haha.

i danced with the devil, and i came out smiling
now i walk in the office and say 'wassup simon'
my life has changed, somewhat drastic
i'm not gonna lie it's fantastic
for far too long i've been eating blue stripe
never complained if it weren't cooked right
the best thing of all
is that i can afford
to foot the bill
at a family meal

The irony in hindsight is the devil took his toll lol! I feel like I paid him in full and I'm not going back. It's a lot nicer living in the light even if that goes against the culture of the times that we live within. The reality is material possessions, quick fame, quick love, quick anything comes with compromise and is built on such flaky foundations that it's hard to ever fully be in control and not being in control of your own life is both horrible and scary and is a time bomb.

Wordart 15-32

Bellyful

i think happy thinks
and i sing happy sings
and i watch what i watch
when i'm watching everything

and i wish that we could
love, love, love them all
with the sound of music
and a bellyful
we could love, love, love them all
when we stand together
then we stand tall
stand together then we stand tall

listen cos this is important:
if i had a voice to the world
tell me, what do you think i should say?
it seems we're all burning in flames
is it time to all just fly away?
but i wish we could dance
and i wish we could play
i think there's still a chance
before it's too late

Stars

when stars start falling
and you want to cry for help
but no one's there to help you
you're all by yourself
everything's at worst
all the things that really hurt
that is when stars start falling down

you have to look towards something
that might not be there yet
you mustn't forget
to look and smile
remember the whiles you did spend
for they were a Godsend

Peace And Love

it used to be to go to school
get a job, buy a house, that we could afford
keep paying it off till we're grey and bored
and then live life on our pensions
now everybody lives at home
with their mum and dad
cause they can't afford their own
they spend all of their money with nothing to show
and there's no long term solution

there's so much to talk about
but nobody talks
they would rather shout
so, you only get heard if you're really loud
and all the madness gets the surface
start spraying their crazy views
and though none of it really applies to you
you can't help but agree with the one or two
and so, you sign up to the circus

there's so much to rectify
everywhere a new ism it could blow your mind
and the timelines make it hard to find
any unbiased opinion
start hating the world i see
but i only hate you cause you hate me
separate myself from any harmony
which causes harm you see, segregation

peace and love and happy stuff i need surrounding me
please provide only good vibes your positivity
i'm waiting for the energy to start an upwards spiral
i'm learning my own recipe the key to my survival

Wordart 15-32

Finding Sobriety

Step one of finding sobriety is wanting to. Being self-aware enough to know that something must change… I'd be lying if I said I waved a halo round my head in one swift tidy moment and change happened because it wasn't that. I'd been aware of my downfalls for some time but living within such a stimulated binge culture of which I am still amongst I was unable to see that I had a problem, unable to admit it, unable to accept it for what it was. Nights out forever feeling like a roulette table; anxiously waiting to find out if i land on being hilarious or a disgrace. But in the wake of self-destruction to my personal life, id grown weary of feeling the cold tongue of being told off by those affected… I was often offered constructive words of support and pointed towards help… AA (Alcoholics Anonymous not the car breakdown company), Church, time away from normality for reflection but I greeted these olive branches with a 'f#*k off, I'm fine' mindset. I am stubborn and don't like to be told what to do. I must find my own paths even if that involves scrambling, climbing, clinging on after I've inevitably fallen on my chosen route…

Change came through being somewhat hoodwinked thinking I was helping a friend out… I knew he'd had substance issues in the past and he called me up to discuss drinking. Specifically stopping and becoming sober. Was it possible? Confronted with challenge something both of us revelled within we concluded of course it is and of course we could do it. I thought he was reaching out for me to support him, but he was talking to me, for me… I guess that's the irony of life sometimes how we are more readily prepared to help other people than ourselves or maybe it's the pride of not wanting to admit or accept that we need help in the first place… Pride is a sin and it works against us sometimes… Shuts us away towards solitude and issues can escalate. Scripture would say that's the devil at play and even a secular tongue would find it hard to disagree. My pal told me about this book; The easy way to control alcohol, Allen Carr… Allen Carr also has iterations for smoking and cocaine… And again, I'd like to say that I listened to my friend and to this book and a magic wand wafted over my life and I was sober… That wasn't the case… I'd be in situations of which id try to make my own rules or take a night off and end up following the same patterns…

Drink driving, getting naked, somehow shit seemed to always be involved and weeing in locations that aren't socially accepted like wardrobes or house plants and harming my body physically. It was either hospital and or a prison cell that was the stick and I started to doubt what the carrot even was anymore because the nothingness, the calming of a black out state whilst piecing life back together no longer had the infatuation that It once held.

At 21 I was famous, my dreams had come true, I was earning good money making music, I had all the possessions I ever wanted, the fame I had craved to silence the doubts I had about self but I was lonely throughout. I had lots of friends and family, but I didn't disclose my inner workings because I don't think many would have understood anyway. 'Write another Lovesick' constantly chiming and yet not happening and so bit by bit i allowed it to all disappear and then what came I wasn't prepared for; I don't think you can prepare for it. The buzz of a sizeable audience most nights, intrigued in your life and work just disappearing and entering a chapter of reworking identity is tough. Will life ever be as good as it once was? Have I peeked already? Am I bound to just being a miserable shadow of self because f*#k that I'd rather out… And I mean that with most sincerity. Youth starts to fade, money starts to run out, hair thins, weight put on. This is why we need purpose. Purpose gives us meaning, something to wake up for and I was too muddied of thought, trapsing through thick gunky swamps in my mind to appreciate anything ahead could be remotely as rewarding as what I'd left behind. Too scared of the magnitude of starting everything again. And so that is why and how I found great confront in being numb. Welcomed the blackout states that alcohol allowed to blanket over and comfortingly sooth. But that is a cunts mentality, it serves only the past and quenches the moment for a moment. We cannot live in the past, we mustn't, it's a nasty trap. We live in a world of abundance and beauty and every day on earth is a gift when you learn to truly appreciate what it truly offers. An ever flowing well of possibility with each waking day.

I learnt that everything Id held in such high regard; labels, status, praise… they are not foundational platforms. They are spice not substance. They are crisps not potatoes. My life started to swirl in a spiral of revelation upon understanding this; I visited my dad in North Wales, one-part heeling our fractured relationship but also the locational escape from the city had a profound impact… Nestled on a peninsular surrounded by sea and mountains they engulfed me and I'd looked out to a raging sea and relished just how insignificant I was. Those mountains have been present well before any Brett lived and will remain well after, the sea continues to rise and claim back land and there is nothing we can do to stop it. We are all just here because nature lets us be amongst it. We chose to pave and build over the earth like it doesn't exist, but we are its subdominant. I started exercising, rearranging social connections to suit the conversations I wanted to partake in and then eventually every time I was operating outside of my values, I would feel it deeply; a physical, emotional response of when I wasn't being authentically myself. Guinness 0.0 was born, pubs started to stock non-alcoholic larger and so I didn't have to be a stranger entirely and everything just felt on track.

I'm not a preacher, I'm not saying alcohol is a demon entirely for everyone although I do think we all have battles with different indulgences. I not saying I don't understand, appreciate, and admire the craftmanship that goes in to aged smoked whisky. What I am saying though is that I didn't have a handle on my life and alcohol became a crutch. This was why I needed change. I was in a battle with my core beliefs and so becoming sober has been one of the best steps for personal growth I have taken and those who love me understand this completely and are proud of me and those who don't, their opinions have found themselves filed in a distant relevance. Boundaries are freeing and allow us to move closer to who we know we are and our overarching purpose.

Wordart 15-32

Alcohol (Myself Lyrics)

i'm not 16 any more,
i can't get pissed up for a score
got loose with a contactless,
wake up with a sore head thinking
"what have i done that for?"
"why can't i just have one?"
all too familiar scenes,
waking up thinking, "shit, what have i done?"
'cause i blacked out and i can't remember a thing
my mate calls me to fill me in,
ohh no, not again
you know, no apology could quite find the words
i'm a nice person at heart,
that's why when i do stupid shit it really hurts
i feel sick, my stomach sinks
i don't have a scooby what i've done and it's baffling
trapped in a wrapping of remorse,
i turn the lights off,
get back in bed
and pretend that it's not happening

all by myself
things start to fall in place and i go and get off my face
all by myself. why me? every time, me

is this all in my head, clean my act up and start again?
i can't wait for this weekend to end
i'm an addict and i've lost the taste for life
i've completely lost sight of what makes me feel nice
i think i'm an addict and i'm not afraid to say
hold my hands up, pack it in, and call it a day
i can't continue with this any more

i don't wanna get too deep, i'm done
temptations all around us and i think it's finally won
how can anyone love me when i can't even love myself?
i'm not asking for sympathy,
i'm just reaching out for help

i keep these feelings to myself
a puppet for my personal demons
and just like that, it all turns grey
looking for a deeper meaning inside of me
a social media world, anxiety's excelled
a cesspit of information to delve
find the right person you can tell
some people bare their souls to people that they barely know
is it good to be this honest? i don't know
i guess a problem shared is a problem solved

i'm getting too old for this shit, man
i just wanna get a dog, put my feet up
and sit by the fire
long walks around the lake, that's nice

all by myself

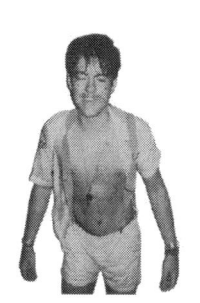

Fame

i must have got lost or confused somewhere along the way
because i found myself peddling someone else's vision
one, i never set out to convey
i guess i longed for that intense injection of success and fame
so much so that when it came
i let it carry me away

upon reflection, that longing wasn't from self
it was to snuff the doubt in everybody else
and like any situation where you find yourself
somewhere you wasn't supposed to be
i got out and so here i am now

knowing what you are not easy
knowing what you are, what you stand for,
that's the hardest part of all
so i went back to the start
back to the boy staring up at the posters on his wall

he had every adam sandler dvd,
even the ones that no one's seen
every iron maiden album because he loved the sleeves
he loved that the guitars made his ears bleed
he loved that the vocals were sung
so he could hum along to the melodies
he loved that with 20 quid in his pocket,
he felt like he had everything
he didn't have to tax and insure his skateboard
didn't have to save up for months to spend the whole summer
down the park and he never got bored
hold tight ridgeway park man, having said this
he did spend a fortune at the ice cream van

i feel like peter pan, reunited with the lost boys
a state of nostalgic adolescence to discover who i truly am
the creative cloud clears from above
and i feel like i can start writing again
not because i have to or because it's what i do
but because it's what i love, love, like forrest loves jenny
like zack loves jessie, like homer loves the telly and sofa
like kel loves orange soda
the creative cloud clears from over my head
and i feel like i can start dreaming again
dreaming, like garth and wayne, sloth and the goons
del boy and rodney, freddy got fingered and his cartoons
and if i end up working in a cheese sandwich factory
for the rest of my life
well, the joke's on you because i love cheese and sandwiches

i'll work hard like billy madison did in first grade
practice like david beckham practiced down at the ridgeway
yep, the same park i learnt to kickflip, he learnt to kick a ball
that shit's inspirational and i'm inspired by my younger self
the boy staring up at the posters on his wall

Hug

is there anything more fulfilling than a hug

sturdy, secure and snug

embraced in arms

it heals, soothes and calms

a moment with someone you love

be yourself

whoever that is

whatever that is

the discovery is a life's journey.

unless you're a lost

in which case aspire to be like someone you admire

Big Ideas Start Small

they are not overwhelmed

they are actioned

little actions, little movements, little motions

repeated again and again and again

recognise your potential

consistency and discipline be your recipe

individual experience offers relevance

let vision be the path of desire

allow imagination to luminate the possible

immerse yourself within the freedom opportunity

meditate, pray and reflect

ensure what you seek is sung with an authentic voice

don't let the fear of magnitude

snuff the desire of a goal

start off small

but always start…

Time

life is not too short

life is great

the decisions of how to spend our time

with the understanding our bodies will change

survival.

reproduction.

harmony.

add to the pot

Wordart 15-32

Bread

there's just something about bread
something in us,
maybe it's the simplistic no fuss
maybe it's the welcoming nature of something familiar
we know and trust
maybe it's a deep ancestral connection woven in our dna
from being a bun in the oven
to numb gums nomming on a rusk as a baby
there's just something about bread.

it's always got us covered
whether it's beans on toast
when there's nothing else in the cupboard
or canapés being doing the rounds
being discovered at a banquette
is there anything better
than warm fresh la baguette

it's one of life's great levellers
served in soup kitchens
or restaurants starred michelin
the experience always equally fulfilling

watch happy faces break bread with friends
and thy neighbours
from around the globe or down the road

with
roti, pitta, chapati, matzah, sangak, focaccia, paratha, challah,
borodinsky, tapalapa, pumpernickel, rugbrød, parāoa rēwena,
muffin, naan, tortilla, beigel, ciabatta, coco, sour dough, arepa
and if
i've missed your favourite tell me and to this list,
i will add it

because i've never met a bread that i didn't get on with
it unites people
and nations
that's flour power
that's how bread rolls
amongst all the bollocks, heartbreak,
and frolics that life tends to throw
just know
you've got all you need and the most
when you sit down with a cup of tea
and a couple of slices of toast
there's just something about bread

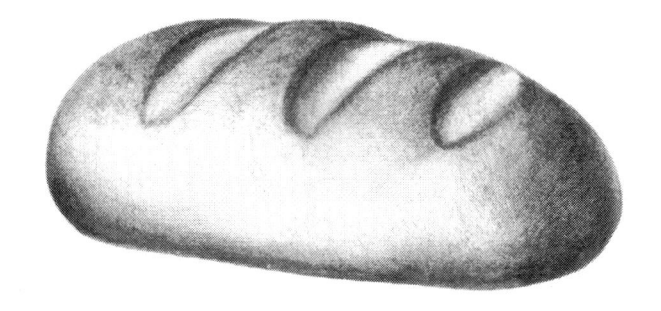

Wordart 15-32

Cooked Breakfast

a quintessential staple for any sensible table
a cosy homely treat
vegan, veggie or meat
large or petit
perfect at any time
on any day of the week
beans, bacon, sausage, tomato,
black pudding, hash brown, 'ave an avocado,
fried slice, eggs twice, chips, toast, tea,
mushrooms, orange juice, freshly brewed coffee,
brown sauce, red sauce – neither either for me
twist of pepper, shake some salt
cheat day's calorie free
with an empty plate guarantee
a beautiful mess of splodge and splash
you can dip it, dab it
mop it, swap it and stab it
the best place to 'ave it – in a cafe.

So, nibble gobble chow
munch polish wolf it down
raise your knife and folk
clang your mug with any old mug
to the hottest meal in town

Wanking

sometimes i feel i need someone
like i'm all alone
and then i have a wank and these feelings go
see i live on my own and smash out wanks throughout the day
but if you knew what i searched for
i'd be banished, exiled and sent away

pregnant, pissing, anal fisting,
hairy, fat, asian, black,
amateur, orgy, squirt, milf,
cum face, cream pie, german filth,
scissoring, british, cartoon, midgets,
double dildo, rimming, vegetables, big tits,
emo, goth, tattoos, pale,
a girl with bloke and another who's transitioning to female

we've all done it... right?
it's usually late at night, the room dark, laptop bright
your imagination; (now he's a dirty sod)
and knows exactly what to do
he's on the think for something new
how many naughty words will fit in one little box?
well, let me tell you the answer is lots
unlimited

and then you crack it and the video starts to buffer
you're about to stream:
'saggy titted grandmas hedge gets dug out by 12 inch lover'
now there's a mouthful (ba dom chh)

your eyes jittery with excitement
because they've never seen this
and they can't keep this news to themselves
so they tell your penis
he shoots straight up like jack's beanstalk
blood rushing all over the gaff
like a dog that's never been for a walk.

and you go from tugging the prick of a dwarf
to needing two hands to climb up canary wharf
wharf for those interested stands for warehouse at riverfront
well this warehouse is where i store my jizz
and you shall do well to remember that abbreviation
because it might come up in a quizzy quizzy pub quiz

i go for it
like a sailor stocking the engines of an iceberg bound titanic
rough
like phil mitchell stroking a freshly shaven vagina with sandpaper
fast
like the relay baton held by usain bolt in the london olympics

keep a keen eye on the video length
at the bottom of the screen
cautious that by now the saggy titted grandma
has had her hedge well and truly dug out
and that the 12-inch lover is about to spit from his spout
my plan is to synchronize our firework displays for all to see
so i pretend i am him and him is me
and proceed on standby ever so gently
like an italian guiding fresh spaghetti

the end is nigh, audience ready to applaud
like a meerkat i search for a suitable lodging for my reward:

- in a sock? it's readily available and relatively easy although it numbs the sensation and your dick might smell cheesy
- in a pair of pants? careful it doesn't fire through the hole for your legs because then it will splat on the wall and that option is next.
- up the wall? the ultimate release, very reckless but if you're renting who am i to judge. now be careful when you wipe it off cause the paintworks known to smudge
- in a condom? if you're feeling posh.
- on your bed sheets? if they're due a wash

- a used t-shirt? is perfect. it dries and is barely traceable within an hour
- on your chest? a no-nonsense approach it washes straight off in a sink or shower

now as i watch with final pumps
pump pump pump pump pump pump pump
explosion noise
apollo 11 launches, the mauna loa erupts
thousands of sperm without an egg or care
my soon forgotten children just fly through the air
infinite potential: lawyers, nurses, scholars, police
maybe the leader of a world that's concurred peace

i hear gasps from the audience
as they watch through their hands
they quickly vote for where they want it to land
the votes have been counted and verified without mistake
and the winner is...

we shall find out after the break.

now, they say that wanking makes you go blind
and i've always wondered why?
for a second i thought i had fell victim to this but...
...i came in my eye.

Wordart 15-32

After Wank

the instant you cum
it stops seeming fun
you lie in your filth
what have you become?
you look at your finger ashamed what you've done
experimentation
lured into your bum
i'm a nice person keep telling yourself
halo disappears
you're going to hell
is it wrong or just frowned upon?
you can't seem to tell
like farting in a duvet and having a smell
or picking your nose and having a taste
if you get caught instant disgrace
maybe i am the messiah
sent to inspire some sheep
a dirty little secret you intend to keep
with conviction
or write it in a poem
and pretend it's all fiction

Vinyl Flooring

peel back the vinyl flooring
and immerse yourself in a time gone by
100 years may have passed
but the purpose and intent does not lie as it still lies
a few cracks and scratches expectedly
but the fact is it still function excellently
and as we purchase and spend
save a tenner here for an ikea wardrobe there
will these even see us through our lifetime?
let alone another's!
so i implore you, as sisters, brothers and cousins.
to think long term
to rummage and mend
fashions change
but classic is classy
and always on trend
so sieve, cypher, beaver, scout
boot sales, charity shops, any open house
peruse and amuse at their collection
for there is stories to be told in every imperfection

Wordart 15-32

Reflection

is this it?
is this all?
is this what forever's to expect?
is there some fairy-tale moment in which happens next?
or is that the insufferable voice of delusion?
because i'm patiently waiting in the wings
clutching the curtain hoping the seams rip
i grab it, i grip
holding on
exposed and uncomfortable
things seem much clearer when vulnerable
without choice a clear path to tread
with age and responsibilities
you become sensible
when did i become sensible?
i knew the role of a drunken fool
but not this
sober i can hear all the haunting voices
projecting fears of opportunities missed
making wrong choices

perspective

my great grandad watched his mates drive over a mine,
blow up and die in a tank
and i'm stressing about which is the better option to take
sucking on for dear life to a triple melon vape
i'm so fortunate
why do i burden myself with doubt
stretch my arms out
receive it, welcome, speak it aloud.
you deserve abundance, make yourself proud

I Can't Get No Sleep

it's late at night when i'm in deepest thought

ideas travel through my imagination

and in my brain they're caught

the pain of remembrance pounds my mind

just hoping i write it down in time

but luckily a well-prepared pen and paper by my side

an arrogant rehearsal foreshadowing my artistic flare

so that now my thoughts are set and stone there

i can clear my concentration and fall asleep

until another idea decides to take a peak.

Snore

you're a snore when i am trying to sleep
a rumbling tummy when there's nothing to eat
an over taking lorry that's going to slow
you're small talk,
asking questions i don't even care to know
you're a drop of lumpy milk
in a cup of tea i've just finished brewing
you're a split in a bin bag
and now my new trainers are ruined
you're a bryll cream gift set when i've got no hair
a corked rifle stealing my shrapnel at the fun fair
which is ironic because there's
absolutely nothing fun or fair
about having the wool pulled over your eyes
you're a goldfish in a sandwich bag
who doesn't feel like much of a prize
you're a sock with holes in on a chilly day
a stubborn dollop of ketchup at the bottom of the bottle
refusing to splat on my plate
you're damp clothes
a stale biscuit
a long sprint to board a train to find you've just missed it
you're a bogey up my nose when people are around
and i can't pick
you're the dickhead standing behind his girlfriend
in a mosh pit
you're brussels sprouts
making me feel like i'm doing a bush tucker trial
you're being contently pissed off

and someone asks you to smile
you lying in bed telling yourself you don't need a wee
when only delaying the inevitable
you're a packet of lurpack butter
with the cheek to call itself spreadable
you're clipboard charity workers
acting like i don't know what you're after
i'm just about staying afloat myself
so i'm not even going to answer
you're a leftover take away in the fridge
that's kept me excited all day
only to come home to discover
your brother has tucked it away
and then he starts telling you how delicious it tastes
he lays his head upstairs
and no amount of horlicks or counting sheep
can musk the snoring when i'm trying to sleep
snore snore snore

Create New Password

he stops to scratch his brain
think of something obvious enough
that he can remember it again
but yet secret enough that no one else can ascertain

sorted! got it! i'll use my go to phrase
it's between 6 - 10 characters, uses both letters and numbers
and involves a capital to make it double safe
clicks enter to proceed ahead
but it stays on the same page
and the writing has turned red

oh, what is it now!
i wasn't looking for a row
i can't be assed this was supposed to be a simple task
ffs!
the peripheral tv making it hard to concentrate
impatience starts to boil up in rage
begins to huff and puff
'password isn't strong enough'

it's 6-10 characters, letters, capitals, numbers
are you sure that's not secure?
i'll remind you tom hanks cracked the da vinci code
the brits created the enigma machine
lest we forget
but no one's logged in as me before
so i'm sorry if i do not share the opinion
that my cypher is under threat

look, i know you mean well
but seriously i can't have another new password
i've already got lots
i get heart palpitations
every time i come across another password box
and besides i'm still confident that the one i've got
is forged as solid as the walls of fort knox

a phrase that could tie rainman's mind up in knots
a phrase approved by appointment to the goblins of gringotts

he stares at the screen impressed with his knowledge of
historic and fictional codes
and although he knows
it still will not comply
he cannot not help but give his go to password another try
persistence doesn't make it right
inevitably it's still wrong the second time
what a farce
shut off by a computerised gandalf
you shall not pass

he has gone too far now to give up on this transaction
turns the tv off to rid external distraction
takes a deep breath, finds some calm
his bullish approach clearly didn't work
so decides to change tack
puts on reading glasses to read the text exact
disappointed his go to password cannot be left intact

four eyes dart from left to right like a pinball
the fonts small so squints
password must include a symbol
like the artist formerly known as prince

he's had enough, that much is true
reluctantly adds an exclamation mark to the end of his go to
and questions whether this is a permanent change
or just a go to to go to too
like a go to two
finally, he is allowed through
and can use the voucher found for deliveroo

This was all a joke…Passwords are important.
Be safe online. Use a password manager.
Lots of good info on the NCSC website.

Wordart 15-32

Internet Mark ii

retirement at 80 jobs centres left, right and centre
queues of optimistic faces sit patiently for their allocated slot
ready for an appointment with their appointed recruitmentbot.

a mature gentleman
taps a young chap lightly on the back of his shoulder
who reluctantly disconnects his virtual headset
to converse with his older.

"did you know that years ago
things were operated by people
and bars were called bars
because of the staff that worked behind them
and phone calls weren't automated
and you could drive things
making music could be a career not just a hobby
and poorer people could work towards owning a property
this isn't me having a moan
i love my smart phone
a world of knowledge
a world connected
i just feel like we never learnt to use it properly
we never found a true balance

there was a brief moment
a small snippet in time
where everyone had a fair,
open and uncontrolled platform to share their minds
an opportunity for the masses to finally unite
expose greed for a fairer share of the pie
but we didn't do that
instead, we used the platforms
and the platforms used us
we argued over minute details
insignificant friction points to fuss

the platforms distanced ourselves from neighbours
we relentlessly watch videos,
silly videos looking for distraction

rather than process challenging thought
and sieve through for any wisdom held
we choose to be instantly offended
in a war of the web wide world
we'd missed the boat
shareholders took control
like everything else
controlled our timelines
controlled the narrative of our minds
and mined our lives for data to sell
and we willingly handed over our entire selves
because it was easier than not
our entire being recorded in long lists
the word privacy was removed
because it ceased to exist
we employed ai's
because they were cheaper than humans
and thus rendered ourselves worthless
we built the technologies that made us unnecessary
it's hilarious if you ask me
anyway, do you know where the toilet is i need a wee?"

E.T. Put Away Phone

i'm bound to my phone
like a dog to a bone
like a home to alone
mary berry to scone or scone
i feel like we're moving forward all wrong
i feel like we've lost the art of conversation
falling out with each other for no reason
welcoming false idols
making careers
preying on those with listening ears
cause it sells
when really these people don't want to help
when really these people are just helping themselves
click bait spreads hate round like a carousel

i'll endeavour to reintroduce analogue methods
wherever apt
and use apps wherever that lacks
be purposeful with time spent on device
less doom scrolling
more being present in life
shinrin-yoku
a japanese practice of being calm and quiet and feeling nice amongst nature,
walking, listening
forest bathing
living not just existing

Moaning

it's easy to moan
but moaning is not constructive
it's just annoying
and annoying eventually fizzles with time and fatigue

but a plan
with clarity
offers execution
something tangible
to stand behind and believe
to be acted upon
and maybe the person in which you first found most disagreeable
might be offered perspective through your vision
and thus be born a productive discourse

lower banners and signs
and raise suggestions, steps and designs
for with that comes advancement
beyond feeling just
and if presentation be greeted with unenthusiastic objection
may the party pushing back
be compelled to improve upon that that exists
and only then be granted a position to criticise
evidence, explanation and action stand greater than opinion
let progress be the fortunate
not personal identity
be humble and graceful

opinions be forged in the fire of individual experience,
sometimes useful, sometimes emotional,
sometimes tainted with bias or agenda
we live different experiences, income, wealth, job title, skill,
education, location, age, interests, beliefs, gender.
so to think we could ever completely agree on anything is a reach
but better is always better
and so to push something forward
position in such a way that ideas are bolstered exceptionally
they'll withstand scrutiny
and offer more than placing burden to the air.

the art of an idea is bringing it to life.

Wordart 15-32

I Don't Care (i always do)

if you don't like my hair
the clothes that i wear
i won't change if you stare
i don't care

if you think that i'm rude
or my jokes are too crude
go hit the snooze
i don't care

your opinions mean nought
will they help me? i doubt
i wont argue or shout
i don't care

i do what is true
to the self that i grew
if that means nothing to you
i don't care

but in here we embrace
for us with similar taste
take a look at my face
i don't care

actually, the reality is that i really do
and with those comments you made my self doubts grew
but the only way that i can continue to push through
is to forcefully conclude
i don't care (i always do)

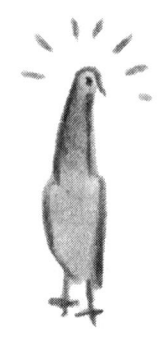

Understand Parents, Understand Theirs

forever trying to understand parenthesis
within them we can unlock our true identities
things are learnt, absorbed
society, teachers, significant others, peers
our parents and theirs
etc, so forth
dna
our beings are partly spoken for before they've even spoken

interview like you're louis theroux
question, prod and poke
love, stoke and provoke
study carefully in hope to gain a master's degree
in your origin story
the family tree
and then just maybe... we can truly begin to understand self
that is our duty
because when people die,
the reasons behind their traumas,
decisions, motives, conquests, failures, successes
die with them
answers die unless recorded
take stock from the egyptians and write everything down!
carve them tales onto the brickwork of your house (joking)

overcompensating behaviours are reactionary
overcome them with awareness
genes mind boggling strands
take the good bits, cut out the fat
grow beyond what we know
elevate through knowledge to become free from our past
and yet somehow become more connected
we owe it to ourselves to truly understand ourselves

one love x

Yonder

the sun that shines selflessly upon my face
the vast ocean flowing
offering a sense of place
navigating through the fog of a crazy life
when all the branches intertwine
in my tangled mind
anchorage i so desperately need
because my sails sail with the slightest breeze
i look back yonder and you are always there
no matter of the what or where
knowing someone is looking out
who loves and cares
i see and appreciate all that you do
may there never be semantic satiation upon saying
i love you

Taken from the historically significant work of Eddie Brett's coming of age explicit fiction novel Odd Herbert. SPOILER ALERT this is a poem that takes place upon Herbert having to recite a poem at his father's funeral.

dear dad,

the many things i wish i'd told you.

there are many things i wish i'd told you,
but these things we don't seem to speak—
how lucky i am to have ever known you;
that's not too silly, i don't think.

it's hard to talk too close to heart,
when trying to seem strong and not distraught,
but, you taught me everything i know —
so if this seems soppy, it's your fault.

we should have had this chat in person,
that's something i now regretfully know,
but i hope it's not too late to tell you,
that i'll be so sad to see you go.

and i'm sorry for all the times,
i gave you reason to tell me off,
i'm a good boy i am, i know i am,
but i can be a little sod.

i don't think distance will ever change
the life long need that i have for you,
nor does your being need to be present,
for your presence to be clear as view.

if this is the last moment that we'll share,
i won't just think this - i'll say it aloud,
the main thing that i wish i'd told you,
is that i promise to make you proud.

i love you dad

Wordart 15-32

Harry Kane

it started in astroturfs
on the playground of primary school
a free for all with a sponge ball
until someone kicked it over
come on man, that's not cool
and you'd have to wait patiently
praying on your knees
for a passer-by,
anyone please
'excuse me geez,
can you kick it over
it's in there amongst the bushes and trees!'

then off to secondary school
the same game, a different ball
as soon the lunch bell goes
straight to the back of the field
blazers and bags for goal posts

wembley doubles
creating and waiting for anything poachable
my toe punts are famous uncoachable
slides tackles that rip trousers
and leave grass stains on knees
absolutely filthy
mum's gonna kill me
i needed to get another day out of these

trials for the school team
a time to unite with your mates
away from the rivalries of sunday league
and i find myself playing for four teams in all
ridgeway rovers
waltham forest
essex county
and chingford foundation school

followed prestigious footsteps
trod by predator boots
david beckham invited me to his academy
when i was 14
because he heard the news
that we'd worn exactly the same kits
and now i can add an england shirt to that list
and a captain's armband of the nation's team

i pinch myself
this is the sort of thing doesn't happen to people like me

i've worked my whole life for this moment
and i won't let it go
to roar and score
it's coming home

Wordart 15-32

Loneliness

lonely
lost
i cling to my pillow for comfort
like a barnacle clings to the haul of a boat
afraid of what the peeling and scraping might reveal
how tender that might feel
there is no perfect solution
i don't think there needs to be a cure
just a battle to wade forward
paddle through the uncertain chopping tide
until i find the unknown that i'm looking for
afraid that even when i do
it'll only be a temporary destination
for i bare the curse of a drifter
rambling
stagnation a puddle under foot
do i powder myself with falsehoods?
brand the restlessness as exploration
optimistic voyaging
do i make a choice?
or am i governed by the fear of being still?
the embarrassment of not being interesting
the shame not being up to something
being dull, yuk
unexceptional, no ta
i'm so far gone normality greets me like an alien
a plague upon its touch
and so, with this a stick i beat myself
a constant pounding for more adventure
lurk in heightened moments of achievement
hide amongst minuscule moments of just not messing up

little steps forward,
just not going backwards is enough
enough for me to be contented
exercise and sobriety a tonic to relent
essential
partnered with the reflective wand of gratitude

i hope you are out there waiting for me,
that shore that i can share my world with
maybe then i won't feel so lonely
but for tonight,
again,
i'm grateful for the comforting hug of my pillow 🖤

Wordart 15-32

Mountains And The Sea

there's something about the mountains and the sea
that brings out the wonder in me
an alleviating injection of insignificance
a thimble blustering through the magnificence of creation
stupendous ore of that that is greater than i
and i smile
for a brief while
any woes and grief
or lies of happiness cloaked within a modern society
seem far away

and i can breathe
deep breaths
lungs full
down pints of this air
go back to the bar for another
because it's so wonderful
and i know it's not corrupt
and i know that it's not been touched
or tinkered by man's evil hand
it's just perfect as it stands
handsome
as it's always been
all sea'y and mountainous'y
blue and green

we do our best to forget and hurt it
rather than appreciate and deserve it
but it will always lend us a sobering reminder
of who's in charge
as it claims back all that we take
and has an unwavering ability to regenerate
but how long must we wait
to respect our pecking order within earth's natural beauty
we dismiss our duty like an unwanted gift
look out to the vast strokes of architectural perfection
and still conclude that it's all chance?
pretend it's no more than uninfluenced consequential randomness?
not on your nellie
we have been blessed

Onlyplans Mars

is sex still sacred
are our bodies our own
does privacy still exist
now we're part human, part phone
or are our bodies marketing tools
to draw in a crowd
do we care what others think anymore?
who do we want to make proud?
are bikini clad pics a quick fix gateway
into a superficial world of onlyfans
is that a shrewd business move or exile to a lonely land
do we need to think beyond a few months towards our future?
or is this a sign that there is no future?
when there's so much to worry about
do we start worrying about nought
cos otherwise it'll weigh you down
so instead why not just get ya dick and/or tits out
worshipping false idols of reality tv hollowness
lives played out in fantasies
i'm sitting at home honoring this
sell sell sell shit shit shit through instagram
and even though i can see see see through all this now
i quite like that tracksuit
so i favourite and cc myself in an email
i can't help but kiss my teeth
it begs belief
who are the role models?
who can be relied upon
when everyone's lying on top of each other?
the cookies monster spying like big brother
how long till we discover it's all wrong
take another selfie in my thong

Wordart 15-32

another thousand likes,
endorphins spike,
heroine needles can't supply that high
what's happened to craft being celebrated,
carpenters, cobblers, tilers, creators
no wonder it's an odd future
what future?
chill dude
it's the best time to be alive
it's just social media can make us blind
to what's worth living for

racism, we won't stand for it,
we'll discuss it
show love
360 conversation delicate and tough
it's important — and that being above
has decided we are the ones to take it forward
to push it over the line.
to bring together a sense of unity or at least try
tick, at least that's something we are doing well
well, at least have started, swell
who can i tell
takes a smug selfie and share with the world

food, wow meat tastes good,
it's just nice
except it's not particular nice is it?
when i think to myself, so i don't think to myself...
but i think about my health and my world
why don't i fall in love with shredded vegetables?
they always make me feel grate
what would it take to take away
the desire for so many takeaways?

i admire those who eat like rabbits
yet i have a habit
for shoving saturated fats down like a gannet
i'm obsessed with processed
i'm out of control man.
it's scary that food gets wasted by the truck load van
yet people are starving?
we take more than we need
we are the world in which we are self harming
more more more
beyond the point it can regenerate
get me to mars
i'm in need of a good holiday

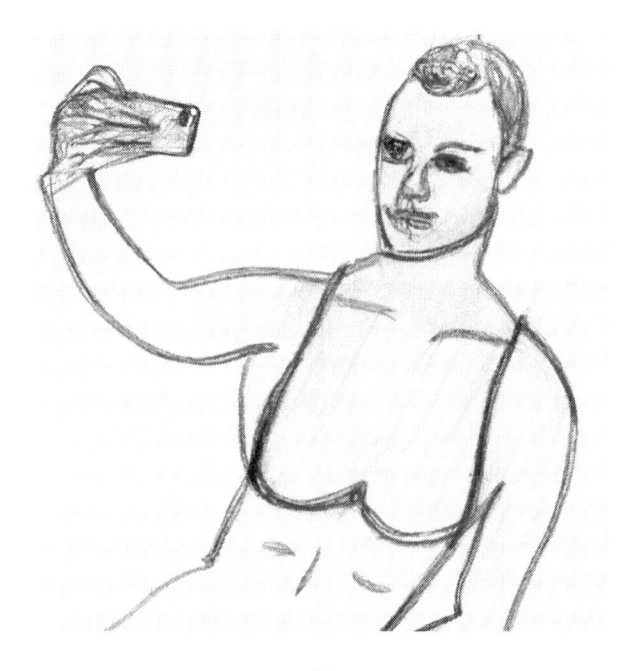

Sinking

sinking doesn't have to be absolute
succumb to the realisation
that we are out of our depth
we may even be drowning
we may be far from home
far from love
far from ourselves
we do not have to freeze within fear
we do not have to fall to the floor without fight.
it is exactly at this moment
during these tumbling crusades
that we must realign
reign in our surroundings
tread precise
cautious
consciously
act
reach out to the few who understand our quarrel and plight
push off from those who absently pull us down with might
we do not have to drown
we are spirited
we can pull ourselves back up

This is a snippet from the yet to be finished musical 'The Tale Of The Cockney Pirate'. I wanted to share to stimulate the creation.

War

there is no tomorrow
we do not live beyond today
history has left us a blank slate
and we demand it remembers our names
we were always the outsiders
the underdogs
the castaways
as they fire musket
we strike sword
as they marry in ceremony
we enjoy broads
as they dine at candlelit table
we dip and munch around cauldron
our knowledge lay stagnant
theirs will live on through children
but we do not hide
we do not shield and retreat
we march on proud, brave, heroic
even in the face of deafening defeat

do not cry with pitied sorrow
do not collapse in fears wretched clutch
but grow strong to face adversity
relish the freedom of knowing we are all royally fucked
this day bares future significance
beyond mortal comprehension
we cannot second guess destiny
but we can ensure legacy never be in question!
nurture your choice tool
live your chosen tale
one last hurrah!
for the time has come
and that time is now!

Wordart 15-32

Have A Drink

you can stay here as long as you like
        as long as we're open
help yourself to whatever you need
        as long as you pay
i see myself somewhat a martyr
        a local samaritan
opening his door to the needy
each and every day

cause if they weren't in here
they'd be out there stealing and fighting
fighting and stealing and stealing and fighting to their death
but in 'ere they're safe from themselves
and i find that fulfilling
i should have knighthood
but i won't hold my breath

so have a drink
just have a drink
when your hearts been struck
you're down on luck
bucket!
have a drink

just have a drink
    come on
just have a drink
    come on
when you're feeling down
and no one's around to tell you what to think
just have a drink

Wordart 15-32

i've seen it all
all kinds of things
i lend an ear
a beer
a tear
some cheer
a fully unqualified shrink
i pour my heart out
when that's all's left to decanter
through the sadness and the darkness
there is bloody good banter
      to be 'ad
cause who wants to be sad
at the end of the day it's night
and we're all born to die right

love can be a stroppy cow
sometimes it needs a little more time
some look for a higher power
find comfort from that bloke in the sky
religions not for everyone
some need just a little more proof
if clarity is what you require
you'll find it after a few
so why not pull up
why not cheer up
and why not join the crew

and have a drink	just have a drink	just have a drink
just have a drink	just have a drink	just have a drink
it helps disorders	what else we got	go ahead and ask
doctor orders	when we have not	we'll fill your glass
join us have a	nonsense have a	quicker than you
drink	drink	can blink

Wordart 15-32

Waltham Forest Borough Of Culture

The borough that I am from Waltham Forest had been awarded 'The borough of culture 2019' a big waste of money to wet the chops of the Mayor before an election. Money trickled into nonlocal pockets. Looking at the positives... There was a weekend of cool performance based art which the community got to enjoy, however at 1 million quid it is all absolutely scandalous. Honestly the way some things are run begs belief but alas we move on. They reached out to local writers and performers, and I was invited to feature in a large light/video display that was projected on to the town hall, my mum and dad used to work in that building so I thought it was quite cool that I'd be blown up across it in video form performing a poem that was pretty much freestyled in the room:

waltham forest, the top shelf of east london
historically part of essex, so i'm told
it's changed a lot round here since i've been growing up
and i'm not even that old...
it's getting a good polish and buff like an old piece of brass
restoring the former beauty of its past
i love it
doesn't take long to be bang in the centre of town
or go the other way and be surrounded
by the breeze, of the green trees...
welcome to the forest

BBC London reported on this event and everything relating the borough of culture and so again they reached out to me to be on the BBC Evening News performing a poem, a different one, they told me I had 20 seconds. I thought 'wow, okay not very long, hmm what can I do?'... I thought about So Solid Crews 21 Seconds song and Romeo's verse... If I did it to that rhythm it would give the piece a recognisable melody and offer some humour to myself knowing that I have 20 Seconds to go. I then thought I could perform dressed up like East 17's iconic Stay Another Day music video for a throwback and nod to the local artists. Between those two themes I was thinking 'GENIUS!', 'this is going to go down a treat'.

Here's the poem:

i've got 21 seconds to go
to tell you about:
leyton, chingford and walthamstow
we've got an historical forest
a painter and decorator called william morris
and you can be in central london
with a short stones throw
we've got david beckham taking over the show
jonathan ives designed the ipod you know
the council is wicked at handing out parking tickets
and gentrification has priced out locals from buying a home

Now, obviously, I was being a bit cheeky with some of the lyrics but that's who we are in East London, and that's who I was serving the poem to. We take the piss out of ourselves, that is our culture, and it was for the borough of culture. Everyone would fully appreciate the humour and honesty, understand the East 17 reference, recognise the So Solid melody and think Eddie Brett was a legend...

However... They cut mine and Leke's (another poet they asked) poems into a mashup of random intertwining couplets... We were absolutely fuming! Poems are whole pieces; they have a narrative that is only fully understood in its complete context and here was the BBC cutting it up themselves without asking permission... This meant that the 21 Seconds melody was no longer, the cheeky humour didn't get aired and I looked like I genuinely rocked up wearing a fluffy white puffer jacket and sunglasses because that's just what I wear. They made an ass out of me. The reviews on Facebook were hilarious.

> John ⬚ Placing William Morris and Augustus Pugin in the same cultural bracket as this pinheaded rapping dirge is an insult to civilisation.
>
> Like · Reply · 5d   1

(It was me that liked that comment lol.)

Seed

everything starts as a seed
whether it shoots out a shaft
or pops from the core of an apple
whether it's a physical thing you can hold
or a magical idea that only exists in your imagination
everything starts as a seed

and that seed's potential must be recognised
it must be respected and nurtured
for it to grow into something
that through the eyes of whomever needs to see it
whomever needs to hear it and understand it
realises its beauty
because beauty starts as a seed

Wordart 15-32

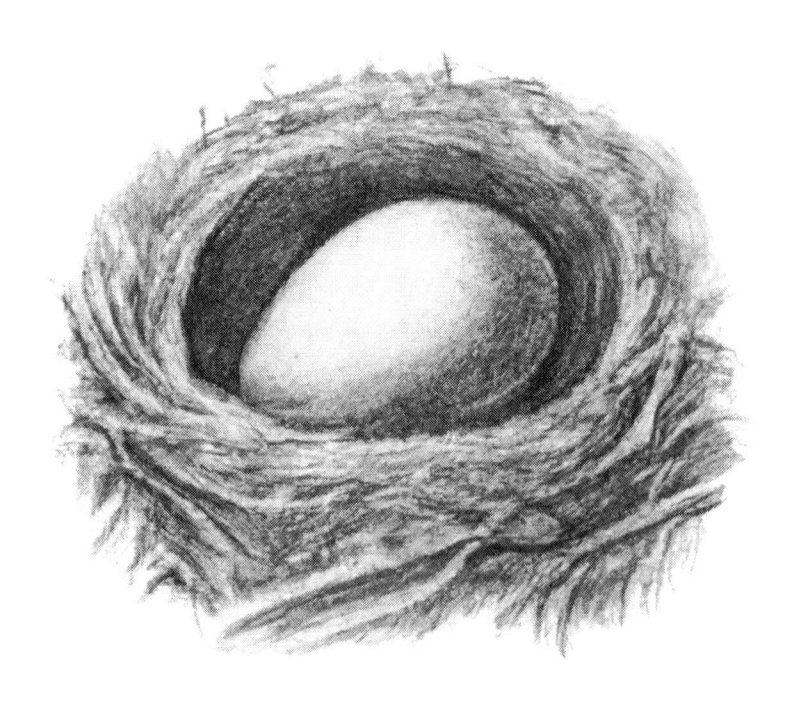

Baldy

baldy, grape, slap head
i suffer from the follicle condition known as an egg in nest
started losing my hair at the tender age of just 23
thought i had years of hair on my head ahead of me
but apparently not
shower by shower
i noticed it was thicker on the sides than it was on top
and rather than morn the decline
of a receding hairline
i thought, d'you know what?
i'm just gonna shave it all off
worrying about what's on your head
rather than in it is no way to live init
it's no way to live
for it's all a matter of perspective
and how many shits you're willing to give
so own it
grow a pair of clippers and embrace them
yes, you will look a bit different
and no, you don't look like jason statham
but get down the gym
by some new aftershave
and become the best version you
i don't want to get too lovey dovey tree huggy
but if someone's not on it because you're bald
swerve them melts
fondue
rejoice with your bald brothers and sisters
for there are some things in life
which we have control of and this is not that
worst case scenario if you still feel like a prick
invest in a nice hat.

Wordart 15-32

Lists

- i like lists.
- a terrible organiser of self
- forever the proud owner of unfollowed calendars
- and empty diaries living on a shelf
- lists keep it simple
- basic, analogue, tangible, stark
- even as i ignore them
- they stay in my mind,
- i can hear them bark
- my pal told a tale of a list he did note
- whilst lost within an unenchanted career
- unaware of where he wanted to go
- he sat down to reflect and a list he wrote
- there are two sides to every story
- and there were two sides to this list
- one side specifics about work he'd rather didn't exist
- the other, welcomed occupational experiences
- but be a realist
- focus on the small important details
- these don't have to be bombastic, far out jots
- it could be to work during school time, near a train station, having a parking spot, or in the city, amongst nature, somewhere tidy, working with your hands
- it's your life, be honest with yourself
- a conscious mind dump to help understand
- how to align with your guts core desires
- thus, allowing contentment within life before it expires
- moments of self-reorganisation can be most profound
- by now, i think you get the gist
- creating your own life direction filtration unit
- all from a clever little list

Wordart 15-32

Wordart 15-32

Love

the one thing you can never have enough
you can feel lost, alone and then everything makes sense
as soon as it comes
it's not about chocolate and flowers
but lending an ear to someone you could talk to for hours
a torch
that shines from the source
increasingly increases the stronger the force
so whore your heart out
ejaculate your emotions
liberate your fond respects
discharge your devotions
love
it's the meaning of life
everything else is just staying alive
and given ourselves things to do to past the time
even if that is just a little while
so love
it starts with a smile

THANK YOU FOR BEING HERE

THANK YOU FOR BEING YOU

Wordart 15-32

OTHER WORKS

FIRST THINGS FIRST MIX TAPE

HONEST EP

THIS AND THAT

THIS AND THAT AND THAT

HE DOES WHAT HE WANTS EP

PARLAY

ODD HERBERT

AUTEUR EGO

THE TALE OF THE COCKNEY PIRATE

Printed in Great Britain
by Amazon

0b5612a6-d8d1-4247-a4b0-97f3ec4f9f2dR01